A PLACE CALLED HEAVEN FOR KIDS

A PLACE CALLED HEAVEN

FOR KIDS

• • •

10 Exciting Things About Our Forever Home

DR. ROBERT JEFFRESS

BakerBooks
a division of Baker Publishing Group
www.BakerBooks.com

Published by Baker Books
a division of Baker Publishing Group
PO Box 6287, Grand Rapids, MI 49516-6287
www.bakerbooks.com

Printed in the United States of America

Library of Congress Cataloging-in-Publication Data
Names: Jeffress, Robert, 1955– author.
Title: A place called heaven for kids / Dr. Robert Jeffress.
Description: Grand Rapids, MI : Baker Books, [2019] | Audience: Ages: 4–7.
Identifiers: LCCN 2018061475 | ISBN 9780801094286 (cloth)
Subjects: LCSH: Heaven—Christianity—Miscellanea—Juvenile literature.
Classification: LCC BT849 .J44 2019 | DDC 236/.24—dc23
LC record available at https://lccn.loc.gov/2018061475

Illustrations by Lisa Reed.

Published in association with Yates & Yates, www.Yates2.com.

19   20   21   22   23   24   25   7   6   5   4   3   2

To my two daughters,
Julia Sadler and Dorothy Jeffress.

I'm proud of you both and remember the time each
of you trusted in Christ as your Savior. The greatest
joy of my life is knowing that Amy and I will spend
eternity with you in that "place called heaven."

Contents

Acknowledgments

No book is a solo effort. I'm deeply indebted to the following people, who were tremendously helpful in creating and communicating this encouraging message to children about "a place called heaven."

Brian Vos, Lindsey Spoolstra, and the entire team at Baker Books, who caught the vision for this children's book immediately.

Derrick G. Jeter, our creative director at Pathway to Victory, who was instrumental in shepherding this book from initial concept to completion.

Robin Crouch, who made sure my words were age-appropriate and could be understood by children, and Lisa Reed, who visualized and created the beautiful illustrations so children might get a better picture of what heaven will be like.

Jennifer Stair, my faithful editor, who provided invaluable finishing touches to the manuscript.

Sealy Yates, my literary agent and friend for more than twenty years, who has always provided sound advice and "outside the lines" creativity.

Mary Shafer, who helped in bringing order out of chaos in the pastor's office.

Carrilyn Baker, my faithful associate for nearly two decades, who helped keep track of the numerous drafts of the manuscript and changes to the illustrations while juggling a multitude of other tasks at the same time—and always with excellence. Ben Lovvorn, Nate Curtis, Patrick Heatherington, Vickie Sterling, Joe Sneed, and the entire Pathway to Victory team, who work hard to share the message of this book with children around the country.

Amy Jeffress, my junior high girlfriend and wife of forty years, who makes everything I am able to do possible.

Is Heaven a Real Place?

Heaven is the place where God lives. It's a special city that God built for you and me. In the middle of the city flows a big river.

Heaven is a real place where everything is perfect. People in heaven are happy. And they live with God forever.

They were looking forward to a better home in heaven. . . . [God] even built a city for them.

Hebrews 11:16 CEV

A river of the water of life, clear as crystal . . . [was] in the middle of its street.

Revelation 22:1–2 NASB

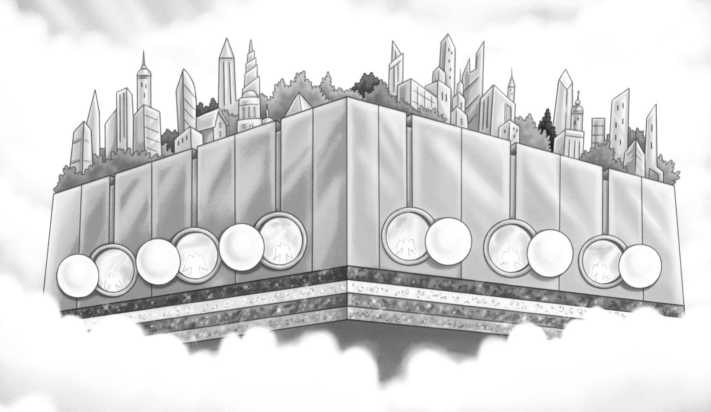

What Does Heaven Look Like?

Heaven is huge! The city is as tall as it is wide. There is plenty of room for everyone who lives there.

Heaven is made of jewels and gold. There is no night there because God gives it light. The gates to heaven are always open, and everyone is safe.

The city does not need the sun or the moon to shine on it. The glory of God is its light.

Revelation 21:23

The city was made of pure gold. . . . The foundation stones of the city walls had every kind of jewel in them.

Revelation 21:18–19

13

Why Is Heaven Called a Kingdom?

God is the king of heaven, so heaven is called God's kingdom. God sits on His throne there and rules over everyone. And Jesus sits by Him.

In God's heavenly kingdom, only good things happen. Heaven is filled with laughter and love because God is a loving and joyful king.

The Lord has set his throne in heaven.
And his kingdom rules over everything.

Psalm 103:19

At the name of Jesus every knee should bow,
in heaven and on earth and under the earth.

Philippians 2:10 NLT

What Will We Look Like in Heaven?

People in heaven have healthy bodies. No one ever needs to go to the doctor or the dentist. And everyone has energy to run and play.

God makes our heavenly bodies brand new. We will never be sad or hurt or tired. And we will never get sick again!

*He will wipe every tear from their
eyes, and there will be no more death
or sorrow or crying or pain.*

Revelation 21:4 NLT

*We grow weary in our present bodies,
and we long to put on our heavenly
bodies like new clothing.*

2 Corinthians 5:2 NLT

Where Will We Live in Heaven?

In heaven, everyone lives near Jesus. Jesus is preparing special homes for all the people who love Him.

"There are lots of places to live in heaven," Jesus said. "I'm going to make a place for you there. I want you to be with Me."

In My Father's house are many dwelling places. . . . I go to prepare a place for you.

John 14:2 NASB

Lord, I love the house where you live. I love the place where your glory is.

Psalm 26:8 NIrV

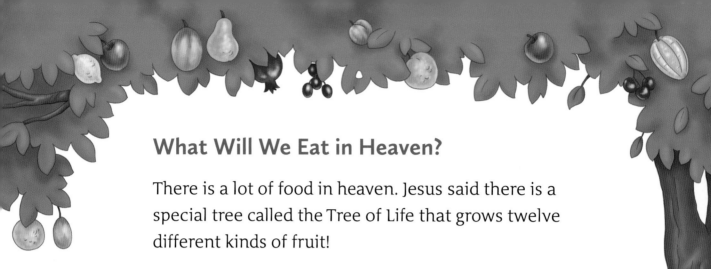

What Will We Eat in Heaven?

There is a lot of food in heaven. Jesus said there is a special tree called the Tree of Life that grows twelve different kinds of fruit!

People will come from the east, west, north, and south.
They will sit down at the table in the kingdom of God.

Luke 13:29

We will have plenty to eat and drink when we sit at God's big table. It will be like going to a birthday party that never ends.

To everyone . . . I will give fruit from the tree of life in the paradise of God.

Revelation 2:7 NLT

Who Will Be in Heaven?

Heaven is for people who trust Jesus as their Savior. Everyone who believes in Jesus will go to heaven someday.

Heaven is filled with people who love Jesus. People from all over the world are there. They all live together happily.

This is how God loved the world: He gave his one and only Son, so that everyone who believes in him will not perish but have eternal life.

John 3:16 NLT

I am the way, and the truth, and the life; no one comes to the Father but through Me.

John 14:6 NASB

What Will We Do in Heaven?

Heaven is God's home. God is good, beautiful, and exciting. Everything is fun in heaven. Nobody ever gets bored.

There is no teasing, only sharing. There are no bullies, only nice people. Everyone is kind to one another because God is love.

> *I am creating new heavens . . .*
> *full of happy people. . . .*
> *There will be no more crying*
> *or sorrow in that city.*
>
> Isaiah 65:17–19 CEV

> *Our only goal is to please God. We want to please him whether we live here or there.*
>
> 2 Corinthians 5:9

Will We Need Anything in Heaven?

In heaven, we will have everything we need. We will have food and clothes and a place to live. We will have friends to play with and family to love.

But most important of all, we will have Jesus.

When Christ appears, we will be like him.
That's because we will see him as he really is.

1 John 3:2 NIrV

[Jesus] will change our humble bodies and
make them like his own glorious body.

Philippians 3:21

How Do People Get to Heaven?

Some people think we have to be good enough to go to heaven. But the Bible says we simply have to trust in Jesus.

To trust in Jesus means to believe that only Jesus can forgive our sins. He said, "Whoever believes in Me will live forever."

I will come again and receive you to Myself,
that where I am, there you may be also.

John 14:3 NASB

I tell you the truth. You must accept
God's kingdom like a little child,
or you will never enter it!

Luke 18:17

A Prayer for You

Do you want to make sure you have a place in heaven someday? If so, you can pray this prayer to talk to God and accept God's gift of salvation.

If you choose to pray this prayer, you don't have to leave your parents and friends and move to heaven right now. But in the future, Jesus will have a home in heaven ready for you.

Dear God,

Thank You for loving me. I know I don't always obey You. I am sorry for the times I sin by doing things that make You sad.

I believe You sent Your Son, Jesus, to die on the cross for me. I believe Jesus took the punishment I deserve for my sins. I trust in what Jesus did on the cross. He saved me from my sins.

Thank You for forgiving me. Thank You for helping me learn how to obey You.

In Jesus's name I pray. Amen.

About the Author

Dr. Robert Jeffress is senior pastor of the thirteen-thousand-member First Baptist Church of Dallas, Texas, and a Fox News contributor. He is also an adjunct professor at Dallas Theological Seminary.

Dr. Jeffress has made more than two thousand guest appearances on various radio and television programs and regularly appears on major mainstream media outlets, such as Fox News channel's *Fox and Friends*, *Hannity*, *Lou Dobbs Tonight*, *Varney & Co.*, and *Judge Jeanine*; ABC's *Good Morning America*; and HBO's *Real Time with Bill Maher*.

Dr. Jeffress hosts a daily radio program, *Pathway to Victory*, that is heard nationwide on over one thousand stations in major markets such as Dallas-Fort Worth, New York City, Chicago, Los Angeles, Houston, Washington, DC, San Francisco, Philadelphia, and Seattle. His daily television program can be seen Monday through Friday on the Hillsong Channel as well as on the Trinity Broadcasting Network (TBN), which also airs "Pathway to Victory" every Sunday.

Dr. Jeffress is the author of twenty-five books, including *Not All Roads Lead to Heaven*, *A Place Called Heaven: 10 Surprising Truths about Your Eternal Home*, and his newest book, *Choosing the Extraordinary Life: God's 7 Secrets for Success and Significance*. He is also the author of two previous children's books: *The Gift: The Gospel for Children* and *The Promise: Celebrating 150 Years of Following God*.

Dr. Jeffress has a DMin from Southwestern Baptist Theological Seminary, a ThM from Dallas Theological Seminary, and a BS degree from Baylor University. In May 2010, he was awarded a Doctor of Divinity degree from Dallas Baptist University. In June 2011, Dr. Jeffress received the Distinguished Alumnus of the Year award from Southwestern Baptist Theological Seminary.

Dr. Jeffress and his wife, Amy, have two daughters and three grandchildren.